Floral Tributes

FOR MODERN MEMORIAL SERVICES

A PUBLICATION OF

florists' review

CONTENTS

WHITE & CREAM

pure and natural,

these colors pay tribute to
a peaceful innocence.

SUBTLE BEAUTY CASKET SPRAY

(left) Pristine white and ivory florals achieve a subtle, untamed quality when combined with grasses, bristly foliages and branches to make this tribute, where a bird appears to have found a quiet place to nest, ideal for a decedent who loved the natural world.

RAMBLING ROSE SPRAY

(right) A trailing crescent of Italian *Ruscus* forms the outline for a pristine palette of white roses, hyacinths, *Scabiosas* and *Veronicas*. A scroll of birch bark imparts a woodsy element, perfect for a nature-lover.

PURE BEAUTY

Lavishly arranged with pure white blossoms, a quiescent wreath, which includes a foam riser in the center, decorates an urn filled with lilies. After the service, mourners can be invited to take a lily from the vase in remembrance of the deceased.

Calla

Veronica

Lily

GLOWING MEMORIES

Downy textures and a glowing candle provide warmth amid cool colors. The arrangement, created in a wreath form, is elevated atop a julep cup and could be arranged in pairs to flank an altar or an urn.

SWEEPING WREATH

(above) Lily grass makes a sweeping sculptural statement in this grand wreath. Swirled among the green- and cream-toned botanicals, bundles of the grass provide a sense of motion.

PERSONALIZED CASKET SPRAY

(left) Traditional in shape but contemporary in style, this casket piece features flowers arranged in groupings, including a lush mound of roses in the center and clusters of line flowers cascading outward. Also grouped are photographs capturing highlights of the life of the departed.

Larkspur

Bells-of-Ireland

Lily Grass

KEEPSAKE DESIGN

(above) Adding a special keepsake to an arrangement, such as this camera, is a popular way to personalize a floral tribute. This curvilinear composition, created with bells-of-Ireland, cradles a prized possession of the deceased, which is nestled in a bed of roses, *Hydrangeas* and novelty *Dianthuses*.

PHOTO MEMORIAL

(right) Coordinating with the casket spray on pages 12-13, this offering also includes photographs chronicling special moments in a loved one's life. The crescent-shaped easel design includes larkspurs and *Dendrobium* orchids to create the graceful linear form while roses and *Hydrangeas* compose the focal area.

Garden-style table wreath

(opposite page) Gardenlike simplicity and beauty are created in this peaceful setting in which stars-of-Bethlehem, *Alstroemerias*, *Nerines*, hyacinths and lady's-slipper orchids emerge from a base of waxflowers, ivy, reindeer moss and variegated *Pittosporum*.

WISPY casket spray

(below) A wispy canopy is created around this spray with delicate emu feather fern that draws focus to the pristine roses, *Cymbidium* and *Dendrobium* orchids, *Dahlias*, and stocks. A base of bundled China millet completes the textural masterpiece.

HIGH-STEPPING MEMORY
(above) This bejeweled high-heel creation is a fitting farewell for the sophisticated woman who enjoyed a bit of sparkle in her life.

CASKET SPRAY ON SCARF
(left) An all-white gathering of fragrant *Freesias,* spray roses and tree fern are enhanced with a fringed drape in this elegant casket adornment.

SOLID GARDENIA HEART

Fragrant *Gardenia* blossoms, outlined by variegated *Pittosporum* leaves, are an elegant offering. Trios of pearl-headed corsage pins affix additional leaves among the blooms, adding subtle shimmer.

Freesia

Gardenia

FRAGRANT OFFERING

A fragrant floral mix of lilies, spray roses, *Phalaenopsis* orchids and feverfew is arranged without foliage, and in a pure white container, to let the ethereal blooms stand out.

PINK & PEACH

warm and welcoming,

these colors honor a beautiful life.

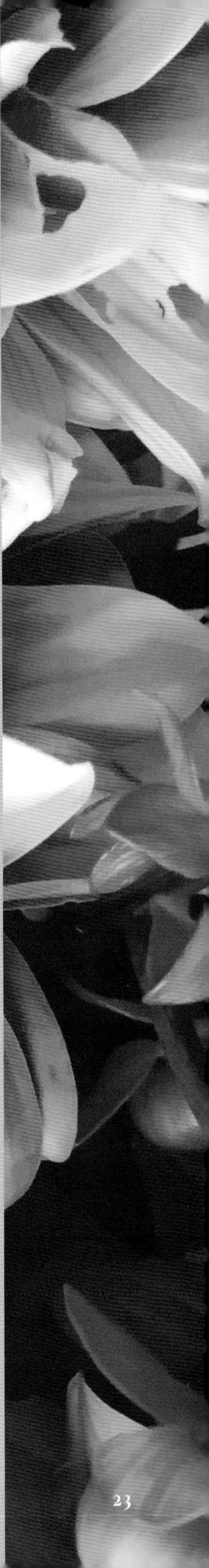

CASKET SPRAY WITH QUILT

Sentimental fabrics, such as throws with inspirational messages or beloved quilts, possibly handmade by the decedent, are popular ways to personalize today's tributes. To fully incorporate this double-wedding-ring-patterned quilt, the casket spray replicates its color palette using cottage-garden-style blossoms.

PRETTY IN PINK

(above) This classic casket piece has a stylish assortment of Oriental lilies, bicolor roses, *Dahlias*, stocks, *Hydrangeas* and foliages wound with silk ribbon for a gentle and tender effect.

GARDEN STYLE WITH PHOTO

(right) A beloved portrait is the focal point of this mix of flowers that appear to have grown up around it, including hybrid tea and spray roses, larkspurs, snapdragons, carnations, asters and *Trachelium*. The setting also would be ideal for a cremation urn.

Rose

Gerbera

HOT PINK HEART

(above) Bedecked lavishly with a wealth of roses and other lovely blossoms, this open heart, accented by sheer lacy ribbon, is the quintessential remembrance for a female decedent.

FLOWER-RIMMED PLANT

(left) Foliage plants are welcome tributes that loved ones enjoy taking home, and with flower enhancements, they can be breathtakingly beautiful memorials.

CASKET SPRAY WITH LIVING PLANTS
Look closely at this colorful mixed-flower casket spray, and you will see *Begonia* and *Kalanchoe* plants nestled in the center. The plants can be removed following the ceremony and given to loved ones as living keepsakes. A variety of flowers and plants can be combined in this manner.

Gerbera

HEART WREATH

(top right) Modern accents of willow balls, dried pods and bundles of carnation stems update this contemporary open heart. *Cymbidium* and *Dendrobium* orchids join roses, carnations and *Hydrangeas* to complete the design.

ABUNDANT WREATH

(right) This lush wreath catches attention with an infusion of midtone pastels – all warm shades of pink, peach and orange. *Hypericum* berries lend textural diversity among the serene blooms. A bow created from softly striped ribbon weaves through the flowers in an intriguing asymmetrical fashion.

PLANTS AND FLOWERS

(left A combination of cut botanicals and plants makes a fitting memorial tribute as the flowers brighten the day and the plants are sentimental keepsakes. This arrangement showcases *Begonia, Echeveria* and lamb's-ears plants with pink roses as the accent, but numerous combinations are possible.

WIRE URN ARRANGEMENT

(right) The weathered wire urn may have been plucked from the garden of the deceased and put on display as a personal tribute. The wiry vessel holds a grand gathering of colorful flowers.

ROSES AND RIBBON WREATH

(below Spiky foliages and vibrant colors combine to memorialize an energetic soul. *Galax* leavesenhance the roses, and the voluminous ribbon adds depth and texture.

PINK & LAVENDER

soft and rosy,
these hues whisper
sentiments of love.

PINK SERPENTINE

Forming an elegant setting for a cremation urn, flowers in a complementary color harmony are arranged in a serpentine-shaped base. Spires of spike flowers rise sporadically from a lush base of assorted blooms and gems while cylinder vases with floating candles become contemporary luminaries.

GARDENER'S BASKET

(left) With garden tools and gloves incorporated into the design, this gentle tribute celebrates a gardener's passion for plants and planting. Cut flowers are arrange into clay pots as if they are blooming plants, and the "plants" are assembled as a collection inside a moss-covered basket

WREATH ADORNMENT

(below) A new take on the classic sympathy basket, this tribute hosts a wreath of garden inspired flowers as the decorative handle.

Rose

FEMININE FAREWELL

(left) In both color and accouterment, this tribute expresses tender sympathies for the loss of a beloved female family member. Gorgeous florals, in a soft mix of pink, ivory and mint, are accessorized by a striking mesh ribbon.

TEXTURAL CASKET SPRAY

(below) This gardeny casket spray is rich with pattern and texture. The bold hot-pink markings of the *Caladium* leaves accent the hues of the garden and spray roses while the cream edges of the variegated *Pittosporum* and ivy reflect each other. Delicate yarrow adds a complementary accent.

DOUBLE-HEART WREATH

(above) Two intersecting hearts symbolize the love of multiple generations. Snow-white roses, baby's breath and oregonia surround the larger heart, to represent the children, and pale pink spray roses cover the smaller, to represent the grandchildren.

FEMININE CASKET SPRAY WITH RIBBONS

(left) Elegant and ultrafeminine, this traditional casket spray, accented with ribbon, is created in layers, with lilies and roses accenting the center. At the base, intriguing foliages impart a sense of strength to the soft palette.

GARDEN BASKET

Gardeny flowers and foliages spill from a moss-and-vine basket, which serves as the foundation of this serene spray. The nature-inspired container, along with groups of greenery, lend a "planted" appearance to the blossoms.

Tulip

Lily

HEARTS AND CHERUBS

(above) For the unfortunate loss of a young girl, this rose-and-*Hydrangea* heart expresses loving sentiments. It is trimmed with boxwood for a "botanical lace" effect, and a pair of cherubs becomes a comforting keepsake.

TOWER OF FLOWERS

(right) Fragrant roses are nestled amid a pillar of abundant waxflowers and *Thryptomene* in a classic container.

DRAMATIC TRIBUTE

Bursting with color and texture, this casket spray offers a mixed aesthetic with rich old-world colors that range from clear pastels to deep hues. Tails of hot-pink burlap ribbon hint at a bow hidden within the coordinating blooms.

HEAVEN-BOUND STYLE
(above) A soothing palette unites this collection of skyward-reaching blooms, from *Liatrises*, carnations, *Freesias*, hyacinths and jasmine branches to heather, *Trachelium*, roses and stocks at its base.

CLASSIC CASKET SPRAY
(left) Incorporating both round florals and spiky stems, this traditional casket spray is ideal for the celebration of a life well lived. This classic style can be reproduced in a variety of color combinations.

ORCHID STANDING SPRAY

(opposite page) This sculptural gathering offers a sophisticated, zenlike quietude with modern accents such as the willow orb and knots of flexi grass. Roses, *Dahlias*, stocks, and *Cymbidium* and *Dendrobium* orchids make up the composition, which extends heavenward with lengths of *Equisetum*.

RADIANT BLOSSOMS SPRAY

(right) Profuse and textural, this abundant gathering of blossoms has a feminine feel with its muted hues. Featured are hybrid tea and spray roses, asters, stocks, larkspurs and *Hypericum* berries in a traditional standing spray.

Stock

Hyacinth

Delphinium

BLUE & PURPLE

cool and comforting,

these shades offer a
peaceful reflection.

ETERNAL LOVE

(above) The long, graceful stems of callas are an important element of this sculptural design as they swirl among their floral companions. Succulents and other plant components provide additional visual appeal, and crimson miniature *Gerberas* offer a departure from the pink-and-purple color palette.

CARNATION TABLE WREATH

(right) A monobotanical wreath of carnations creates a textural tribute for a cremation urn. The dense arrangement of the cream-tipped, ruffle-edged blooms makes a luxurious presence.

FLEMISH FLORALS

(right) Reminiscent of a Flemish floral gathering, this formal arrangement will make a stately presence at a memorial for either a man or woman. Foliage accents offer contrast in texture, color, size and form.

WREATH WITH SASH
(above) This striped ribbon is placed unexpectedly across the center of this mixed flower wreath like a sash, giving the classic shape a modern look.

BLUE AND LAVENDER CASKET SPRAY
(left) Ranging from pale blue and lavender to regal violet, this analogous collection has a comforting quality and is appropriate for both male and female decedents. A simple tie of pretty purple burlap ribbon adds a bit of casual charm to the garden-inspired blossoms, suggesting this tribute for a stylish person with down-to-earth demeanor.

Lisianthus

Hydrangea

China Aster

LUSH ARRANGEMENT
IN RUSTIC URN

In accordance with the calming color palette, the weathered-looking urn, complete with faux cracks, imparts a sense of nature's serenity.

LEAF-TRIMMED HEART

(right) Multiple chrysanthemum varieties form a sweet heart shape accented with salal leaves and a gauzy ribbon.

CASKET SPRAY WITH HEART

(below) Lavender button spray chrysanthemums and *Leucadendrons* make up the heart at the center of this spray. Coordinating roses and waxflowers add ancillary hints of color amid a textural framework of *Spiraea*, lily grass and bracelet honey myrtle. Pale green gems enhance the mums' centers.

BOTANICAL CATCH

(above) A fish-shaped form is covered with moss and juniper, and the "petals" of a disassembled succulent are arranged into the foam to resemble scales. The fish can be positioned on an easel near the casket, so the hook can be secured in its "mouth."

FISHERMAN'S TRIBUTE

(left) In celebration of a loved-one's life, family members often choose to incorporate a decedent's personal effects, especially those related to a favorite hobby or pastime. Here, a fisherman's rod and reel are secured into a casket saddle while a florally interpreted fish is positioned to appear on the line.

Eryngium

Wheat

Delphinium

LILY CASKET SPRAY

(opposite page) Fully opened lilies offer solace within this comforting casket spray that incorporates lilies, Belladonna *Delphiniums*, *Eryngiums*, *Hydrangeas* and green wheat.

FABULOUS FAN

(right) Boasting a simple yet stunning explosion of *Delphiniums*, this composition offers a contemporary take on a symmetrical arrangement. *Hosta* leaves and two types of ferns offer verdant punctuation to the blue-hued blooms arranged in asimple container.

URN ENHANCEMENT

(below) Though small in stature, the urn is elevated to a position of prominence amid a harmonious palette of analogous colors – from yellow-green *Hydrangeas* to green *Trachelium* and *Dianthus* to blue-green *Eryngiums*.

CRYSTAL CROSS

(above) An elegant cross, which can become a cherished remembrance for family members, is a central feature of this design. A traditional shape and simple color palette contribute to its consoling qualities.

BLUE CASKET PIECE WITH YELLOW ROSE NOSEGAYS

(left) A trio of sunny yellow rose nosegays can represent significant family members, like three loving daughters. The compositions are arranged among similarly mounded *Hydrangeas* and *Trachelium* as well as linear *Delphiniums* and foliages. The blue-and-yellow color combination adds to the dramatic effect of this spectacular casket piece.

Delphinium

Trachelium

Ranunculus

CASKET SPRAY WITH CHRYSANTHEMUMS

Warm yellow spider chrysanthemums and *Solidaster* stand out against the blues and greens of the Belladonna *Delphiniums*, *Hydrangeas*, and *Fatsia* and croton leaves. The veins in the croton leaves continue the pattern created by the *Solidaster*'s form.

SPRINGTIME SPRAY

(right) Groupings of roses, *Alstroemerias*, *Hydrangeas* and *Solidago* nestle into graduated sizes of willow baskets to create a standing spray accented with 'Green Trick' *Dianthuses* and salal leaves. An egg-filled nest completes the natural collection.

YELLOW & ORANGE

bright and beautiful,
these vibrant hues celebrate
a life well lived.

EARTHY ARRANGEMENT

(below) Mossy elements and a weathered vessel contribute a wetlands feel to this masculine tribute, which includes lilies, Queen Anne's lace, birch branches and assorted foliages and dried materials.

FIELD OF FLOWERS
Leaves form a botanical "bow" at the base of this tribute that resembles a field of mixed flowers. A sturdy urn adds weight to the frothy flower arrangement.

URN WITH FLOWER RING

This flower ring features *Dahlias*, roses, hellebores, miniature callas, *Solidago* and swirls of broad foliage for a stunning way to highlight the ceremonial urn.

CASCADING CASKET SPRAY

(above) Dramatic variegated *Aspidistra* leaves are formed into a large living "bow" accented with a cascade of spider chrysanthemums to make a small and sleek casket spray.

ORCHID ARRANGEMENT

(left) Simple but elegant, this abundant arrangement of *Cymbidium* orchids and looped steel grass is a long-lasting and easy-to-transport option for honoring a loved one.

Rose

Solidago

Chrysanthemum

MIXED YELLOW WREATH

A monochromatic collection of roses, spider and spray chrysanthemums, *Solidago*, and salal leaves is bursting with sunshine in this classic wreath offering.

STATELY SPRAY

This elegant standing spray is finished with radiating *Aspidistra* leaves, some of which are looped for a bowlike effect.

TALL FLOWER BASKET

Roses, carnations and spider chrysanthemums appear to grow past the confines of this customary arch-handled basket.

FLOWER-DECORATED CROSS

This memorial offering achieves a multidimensional effect in which a faux-bois cross appears to be laid into a bed of golden flowers. Yellow is the most luminous and uplifting color in the spectrum, and it captures people's attention more than any other hue.

GOLDEN COMMEMORATION

In almost every culture, yellow represents happiness, making it the ideal color for celebration-of-life florals. Enhancing the vibrant, sunny florals that surround this cremation urn is the visual movement created by curved stems of sago palm and accentuated by the wavy stems of snapdragons.

Sunflower

Snapdragon

URN ARRANGEMENT WITH SHEAF

(below) Traditionally, sheaves of grain have symbolized the rich harvest of a good life. Roses, spray chrysanthemums, carnations, *Hydrangeas* and seeded *Eucalyptus* make a verdant base for the foxtail millet and birch twigs at this arrangement's heart.

COLUMNS OF FLOWERS

(above) Strong groupings of flower types and colors create dramatic impact in this arrangement. The striking columns of snapdragons and bells-of-Ireland seem to be reaching for the heavens but are grounded with a tight grouping of pincusions at the base of the urn.

CASKET SPRAY WITH WREATH

Amber grains, golden sunflowers and verdant bells-of-Ireland spring from a wreath of dried and preserved florals atop a base of *Aspidistra* leaves, creating a field-gathered look. The natural wreath can be kept as a remembrance after the services.

ORCHID WREATH

(above) The colors of the lush foliages are repeated in the hue of the orchids' throats, resulting in a peaceful and harmonious tribute.

EXOTIC CASKET PIECE

(left) Stunning orchids and exotic foliages, along with roses and callas in a sun-drenched hue, pay tribute to a person who loved island destinations. Sprays of long-lasting *Cymbidium* orchids add a regal touch, and can be removed a given to a loved one after the service.

BOTANICAL CROSS

With its heavy use of foliage and rich autumn colors, this botanical cross is suitable for honoring the life of a dynamic man or woman. Ti and flax leaves alongwith river cane form the cross itself, and roses, red and deciduous huckleberry, seeded *Eucalyptus*, and *Leucadendrons* create the gorgeous ornamentation.

SUN-DRENCHED URN ENHANCEMENT

(right) A wreathlike arrangement, in an uplifting color palette, provides a floral accent for a stately cremation urn. Crisscrossed blades of lily grass add modern dimension to the memorial.

SOARING LILY BASKET

(below) Reaching approximately three feet in height, this captivating composition features bold coral-hued lilies, orange *Asclepias* and sword fern in a woven basket.

Rose

Cymbidium

REDS & SERVICE TRIBUTES

rich and respectful,

these colors honor those who have given unselfishly to others.

BANDED WREATH
(above) Flowers arranged in monobotanical bands around the wreath form, and then finished with an earth-toned ribbon, give this remembrance a distinctively masculine feel. By selecting different color combinations, this style could be adapted for a woman.

VIBRANT CASKET SPRAY
(left) Most appropriate for men, this intensely hued floral option offers solace during the summer and fall months. Bold colors and varied textures combine to make this casket spray especially impacting.

NATURE'S BEST

This memorial tribute, with a gilded crematory box at its center, features flowers arranged in separate groups that, together, resemble a loved and cultivated garden.

Hypericum

Hydrangea

TREASURED KEEPSAKE
(above) When fresh flowers are combined with a keepsake, like this sentimental angel statue, the family has a lasting remembrance to take home after the service.

CLASSIC CARNATION CASKET SPRAY
(left) Carnations are a classic flower frequently used in sympathy work; they are affordable and long lasting and frequently have a spicy-sweet fragrance. Here, red carnations are accented with white *Lisianthuses*, larkspurs, *Astilbe* and dusty miller foliage. Carnations are readily available in a wide variety of beautiful solid colors and bicolors, so a tribute can be personalized in almost any color combination.

SCALLOP-HANDLED BASKET

(opposite page) An impressive arrangement such as this is achieved by using an affordable handled basket and a combination of both spike and feature flowers. Again, carnations provide the color and are accented with larkspurs, *Lisianthuses* and Queen Anne's lace. A quality ribbon treatment with jeweled accent provides a touch of elegance.

CLASSIC URN

(right) For a more masculine treatment, select a dark-toned urn and a spray of green wheat to add weight and height to a classic carnation arrangement.

WICKER REMEMBERANCE

(below) A warm-toned basket provides a solid base for an arrangement of red carnations, 'Green Trick' *Dianthuses* and *Eucalyptus* sprays. A sheaf of wheat and a twist of rustic wire provides an agrarian accent.

Carnation

Lisianthus

Dusty Miller

SERVICE TRIBUTES

Celebrating the lives of those in service to a city, a state or the nation, from military members and veterans to first responders and public servants, these patriotic tributes are more dramatic and exude a quiet strength, in part, because of the grouping of flower types and colors.

VASE OF ROSES

(above) A classic vase of red roses is a welcome gift at the service or home of a loved one.

RED, WHITE AND BLUE CASKET SPRAY

(left) Clustering flower types and colors enhances the drama of this patriotic-themed casket spray. Diagonal groupings of blue hybrid *Delphiniums* and white *Dendrobium* orchids draw visual attention to the heart made of red roses.

Delphinium

Rose

Gladiolus

SEAL OF SERVICE

A horizontal spray of *Dendrobium* orchids provides a lush base for a military service seal encircled with red carnations. Many seals can be located online, including those for military branches, government departments and even schools, then the digital files can be emailed to a local print shop for reproduction in any size.

WREATH OF ROSES

(above) A circle of red roses and ivy is one of the most enduring symbols of never-ending love. Wreaths can be made in sizes small enough to be tucked inside the lid of a casket or large enough to decorate the entrance to a mausoleum.

FLAG OF HONOR

(left) This vertical urn arrangement was designed to respectfully showcase a folded U.S. flag. Standards set forth in the U.S. Flag Code, as well as precautions for preventing damage, limit the ways flags can be displayed, particularly in floral designs. This floral tribute of white *Gladioli* and red roses was created to incorporate a flag, which is put in place at the service. The cremation box is decorated with a patriotic emblem.

THE SIGNIFICANCE OF

FLORAL TRIBUTES

Sympathy for the loss of a loved one can be expressed in a variety of ways, and one tradition that has been part of nearly every culture throughout history is the sending, giving or use of flowers. Both consumers and professionals in the floral and funeral industries witness how flowers and plants provide comfort to families and add beauty to ceremony settings. The options for floral tributes are as varied as the people who order them and the florists who create them. Today, the trend is to create personalized floral arrangements that capture the spirit of the departed. There are dozens of photographs in this book to provide ideas, but your professional florist is trained and experienced to create something perfect, just for you.

TRIBUTES

Flowers that have a special meaning for the deceased and/or the family are especially popular. Many people like to incorporate something meaningful with the flowers, like a memorable photo of the loved one or a treasured quilt lovingly made or owned by the departed such as the one draping this casket.

KEEPSAKES

Incorporating keepsakes with sympathy flower and plant designs provides a tribute now, and the items will become cherished remembrances for years to come. Consider items such as figurines, religious symbols, memorial stones with personalized inscriptions, engraved plaques, memorial ornaments, flameless candles with inspirational messages, afghans, wind chimes, photo frames, treasure boxes and more.

AFTER THE SERVICE

Family members often take home many of the flowers and plants that are sent to services. Other times, floral arrangements and plants find a second home at elder care or similar facilities. Some people find comfort in crafting flowers into lasting memorials. Once dried and pressed, sympathy flowers can be incorporated into shadowboxes, domes, holiday ornaments, rosaries, jewelry and so on.

PLANTS

Flowering and foliage plants are welcome gifts and almost always taken home by family members. Some people keep the plants for many years and even divide and share them with other family members, as they grow larger. This tribute contains both a foliage and blooming plant with a keepsake bird in an elegant container.

CLARIFYING "IN LIEU OF FLOWERS ..."

Many people misunderstand the phrase "In lieu of flowers ...." It does not mean that the family of the deceased refuses to accept sympathy flowers; rather, it intends to suggest alternative options for how mourners should offer condolences, such as making memorial donations. Families and funeral directors can help prevent confusion by using more clearly worded phrases for obituaries. The following phrases honor requests for charitable giving but do not demand how mourners should express themselves.

- Memorial contributions can be made to ....
- Should friends desire, contributions can be sent to ....
- Memorials can be made to the charity of your choice.
- The family has designated ... for memorial contributions.

photo: iBulb

Some information was referenced from a report released by the American Floral Endowment (AFE) and Floral Marketing Research Fund (FMRF) entitled "Funeral Directors and Flowers – Insights into Floral Tributes in the Floral Industry"
To get your free copy of this report, visit www.fmrf.org, create a free account (or log in to your existing account) and download the report in its entirety.